andrea &
hannah.

YOUR PRECIOUS
HEARTS WILL CHANGE
THIS PLANET
Follow what _feels_
best. ♡

Lauren
zung.

73

PS. Corniness
comes with theroad.

The Smell of Good Mud
a collection of poetry

ভ

by Lauren Zuniga

WRITEBLOODY
QUALITY AMERICAN BOOKS

Write Bloody Publishing
America's Independent Press

Long Beach, CA

WRITEBLOODY.COM

Zuniga, Lauren.
1ˢᵗ edition.
ISBN: 978-1-935904-97-7

Interior Layout by Lea C. Deschenes
Cover Designed by Gary Musgrave
Proofread by Zhanna Vaynberg
Edited by Derrick Brown, Courtney Olsen and Stevie Edwards
Type set in Bergamo from www.theleagueofmoveabletype.com

Printed in Tennessee, USA

Write Bloody Publishing
Long Beach, CA
Support Independent Presses
writebloody.com

To contact the author, send an email to writebloody@gmail.com

MADE IN THE USA

To Kavi Moon and Briam Sky. One day, we will go on tour and do nothing but swim in hotel swimming pools and take pictures of abandoned barns. Thank you for your patience.

THE SMELL OF GOOD MUD

THE SMELL OF GOOD MUD

FLATLAND GOSPEL

TRY SURRENDER.
SEE WHAT HAPPENS.

OPENING

The photographer says she can't wait until my next opening.
I start to correct her and say, *with poetry,*
it's called a reading, or a performance,
sometimes a slam.
Then I realize maybe that's the problem.
I step on my loud and say,

Yes. Please come to my next opening!

It will not be all good light and gallery smiles
but I will fresh slice the walls for you,
hang my absurd and wait for the wine to spill.

It's been a long time since I've shown anything.

Notice the ten-foot installation of Talks Too Much.
I eat margarine when I'm nervous. I get nervous
when you like me. I describe things poetically
to keep from saying what I really think.
This one here is my father. Notice his head
asleep on the stove. His hands, bloated livers.
I drink when I can't decide who to be.
I starve when I decide I'm too much. I am angry,
almost never.
Which means you best prepare yourself
for the nasty awkward that will rain down upon you,
when I decide some things deserve my fucking angry.
I fall in love like some women fall in mortgage.
I have damn near become my mother
minus five husbands and a bad case of arthritis.
I am still cracking knuckles and divorcing.
Here's a ticket to The Moment I Surrender.
A portrait called I Don't Know Anything.
I am terrified that my children think I love poetry
more than I love them. I am never alone. Never ever alone.
I go to crowded places where we sit, with a small plate
of cheese and fruit, cock our head to one side and say,

I can't believe someone pinned my stomach to a canvas.

That is why we do this.

This is an invitation to stop swallowing the art in your mouth.
This is an invitation to stop ripping yourself apart.
This is an invitation to be a live nude. Let them draw you
dirty, flawed and glistening.
This is an invitation to
your opening.

CLEMENTINE, THE HOUSE.

"Together we work to expel the bore-ocratic chairman of the bored. We strive to make the world Weirder."

— Mary Daly

TUESDAY EVENING

Talia pots the citronella to keep
the mosquitoes away. Hangs the mirror.
Waters the rosemary. The tape player
offers muffled trumpet, backyard clarinet.
Keeps time with the curtains slapping
their knees against the window.

The kids are lined up at the corner
waiting for the ice cream man.
Pink headband gang. Drumsticks
in back pockets. Silver coins drop
from hips. They know their loot
will go into the freezer until after dinner
but the little ones giggle, nervous,
as the big ones count their change.

Penny slices onions and the freshest
block of tofu. Megan scoops
spaghetti squash in yellow mounds
of ribbon. Chickweed and dandelion
salad. Sprinkle of sunflower seeds.
Wild rice and morel mushrooms.

The girls built the raised bed while
I was at work. Cedar planks, a truck
full of black dirt. I staple chicken wire
to the wood frame for the compost bin.
The staples punch like snare.
The breeze sings like a plastic harmonica.
I fall in love a thousand times before
I ever get called into dinner.

GAS STATION VODKA

Maybe it was the gas station vodka and Tahitian Treat.
The bottle rockets exploding in the subway parking lot.
Maybe it was the man in white pants punk-singing
in the basement. The astronaut on the amp,
the green umbrella, the ukulele.
Maybe it was the tough and lovelies haunting
the turn table. The red shag carpet, the rooster lamp.

When I looked at you in that vinyl evening,
I decided then and there that we really should
get that cottage.
Our cottage should not be in the woods, though.
It should be in the city. With a yard full of goats
that sing us worship songs.
We should have a puppet theater with a tiny
green dressing room for our puppets.

We need a huge comfy couch where our feet
don't touch the ground. It will make us feel small
when we get too big for our britches. And we will.
Get too big for our britches. We will get terribly
lonesome in our fame. We will get so deep
in our awesomeness that we won't even
be able to see how awesome we are.
We will need each other.

We will need a room full of compasses and stopwatches.
Otherwise, we will have no idea where we are or how long
we've been there. We will say *Thanks* every time we leave
the bathroom. We will drink, gossip, and curl lips like old
people who don't give a damn about anything because
they are old. But we won't ever get old. We will get artistic.
We will get Grand Canyon and shoreline. We will get naked.
A lot. We will be jars and jars of kisspulp and the goats
will lick the kisspulp from our lids and you will say those goats
are so damn gross and I will say maybe we should sell the goats
but keep the puppet theater. I promise it will be really beautiful.

Maybe it was the gas station vodka and the Tahitian Treat.
But in this light, our story is so delicious.

DEAR LEMON ENGINE

My grandmother's hands don't work anymore. They are twisted seashells. She keeps every ex-husband on her back. Secretaries. Stillborn babies. Dried up milk. Keeps them in the floppy pockets of her nightgown. Let's them gnaw on her bones. I don't want to be crippled.

Sometimes when I walk to my car after work, a little switch goes off in my brain that tells me to find all the anger in my body and release it. It feels like a tight spool of thread unraveling. The anger in my spleen, liver, ankles, is always some little thing I picked up. An impulse purchase.

Anger didn't start out as anger. It was neglected as a youth. Locked in some back room until it emerged with spiked hair and heavy, safety-pinned jeans. Some days, it is one tough little punk.

I've noticed though, that when I take a moment to acknowledge it, call it by name, it dissipates. It floats away like the end of a song. Maybe if I could get quiet more often, I would notice it before it became a punk. Before it wreaks havoc on my bones. Before I launch it at some unsuspecting person and throw my hip out.

When I am seventy, I want to be in Bali or India. I want to wear long flowing tunics and grey braids. I want to kiss your forehead, drink Tulsi tea in the afternoon. You are younger than me. Spry wisp you will be. Playing banjo in combat boots, making out with grocery clerks. We will giggle when we tell stories about the house we named Clementine. How you held me by the crape myrtle and said, "Loving yourself is the greatest revolution."

I wish I knew how to move slower. How to kiss hard and still come up for air. How to be kind to each moment like it is my very best lover, an engine of pumpkin sweat and skin. I hope I learn to love myself when no one is looking. I need to drink more water. Maybe that is all I ever need to do. Drink more water. Kiss you. Walk to the store. I am the slowest revolutionary.

Holy Chicken Coop, I can't wait to move in.

THE NIGHT WE PLUCKED ONE THOUSAND PRICKLY PEAR BURRS FROM HER ASS

was strangely erotic. Each time the tweezers
grabbed hold of a small stinging ghost,
her butt cheeks winced and the backs of her thighs
tightened, like the nervous flinch of a first kiss.

It had to be arousing for her too. To be sprawled
naked on the chaise, each freckle pierced,
our fingers eagerly rubbing her skin to feel
for its sharp shadow.

As we worked,
we laughed about the epic headlock,
the cackling boys, the collapsing bush.
PBR cans strewn across the lawn,
fireworks shaking the horizon like the last grimy
hour of a warehouse rave.

We never outgrow explosion.

We bitched about how our cycles
had been forced into each other, how
blood in the compost heap seems
to attract animals, how we've forgotten
we are animals and how he will never really
love her.

We do not talk about how we found her.
How we could hear the guttural sobs
all the way from the living room. Hot shower
only rinsing the sound. A porcupine curled up
in a thin stream of mascara. We just pluck—

as if each burr were a moment of pain,
caught, wiped on the warm washcloth
and replaced with the forgiving lust
of friends.

HOE, PLOUGH

"Where females work the field
with a hoe, God is a woman.
Where males work the field
with a plough, God is a man."
— Ken Wilber, Sex, Ecology, Spirituality

It took four days and everyone
in the house to finish the mound.
What started in the shape of a C,
soon became a lopsided uterus
or maybe a filthy vulva, making
the thrust of shovel into frigid
ground hilarious.

When the hole was hollow
and thirsty, we filled the wagon
with cocoa-rich compost, lifted
together, watched it tumble
like the thick, unused wall
of a womb. We planted
strawberries and zucchinis.

I've never made so many
sex jokes in my life.

I never noticed the shape
of the moon before.
How my cycle shifts
from full to new when I
work this dirty for food.

CIRCLE DRIVE

My neighbor just came out to her husband. They have been married for fifteen years and have three daughters. She has been in love with the same woman for five years but never once touched her skin. Never had the courage to explore the terrain of her sex. Terrified of what the neighbors would think.

Her neighbors are a rowdy house of queer women. They light bonfires and erect giant maypoles to celebrate the fertility of spring. They occasionally kiss each other. They sleep on the roof. They want a chicken coop but roosters are noisy and messy and illegal in the city. The neighbors might call the code enforcer.

The code enforcer lives across the street. He eats pastrami sandwiches every day and loves Bon Jovi. His wife is a dominatrix that he refers to as *Mistress*. She mows the lawn wearing black leather. Their boyfriend sleeps in the garage and works as a hair stylist. If he told his parents about the living arrangement he would be disowned.

His parents are retired and enjoy gardening and horseback riding. Recently, the mother has been wearing leopard print aprons and lace panties when she cooks. His father likes to have sex with her against the stove. She wants to scream until her grandmother's china shatters in the cabinet. She doesn't. She is terrified of what the neighbors will think.

CHISLERS

1.

The fingernails in the welfare office sashay
and bling like the swimsuit portion of a toddler
pageant. They express deep support for sports
teams and holidays and various wildlife.
They clench jeweled cell phones, pacifiers, utility bills,
and last week's check stub with dazzling grace.
I feel underdressed in my well-bitten nubs
and therefore snobby. My mouth begins to twist
the way the clerks did when I used my food stamp
card to buy organic produce at the health food store.

2.

During the Emergency Relief efforts of the 1930s,
social workers giving aid were instructed to beware
of *chiselers living in sinful luxury*. Before granting aid,
the caseworkers visited homes, catalogued
every single item, determined whether there was
genuine need. The recipients were also required a certain
level of grooming, including regular baths, clean teeth,
trimmed hair and manicured nails. An unkempt female
was potentially a prostitute and therefore undeserving
of government help.

3.

In cosmetology school in 1996, the length and decorative
painting of your acrylic nails tells everyone who you are.
If you think of yourself as a good girl but still want to
appear fuckable, you wear mid-length French manicures
with occasional opalescent or delicate flower designs.
If you are an edgy girl with fat cherry streaks in your hair
and tough, laced boots, your nails are inch-long black stripes.
If you are a Chola with perfectly penciled eyebrows who sits
in large packs laughing, saying *Jaiva* to the white girls
then you have nails as long and ornate as a bouncing Chevy
Impala.

4.

In the community garden, we eat big bowls of freshly picked
greens. When finished, I watch my friend wash her bowl
with a small cup of water. Her dirt-caked nails swish and slip
inside the bowl in a careful ceremony. She dries her hands
on her salty hairline and asks how I'm holding up without
a job. I tell her I have to renew my food stamps tomorrow.
My face powdered in shame. She says, *Cheap, nasty food
is all we can afford because the government subsidizes it.
Is it wrong to let them subsidize you?* I nibble on the last
of my dinner. The sun is a glowing *Open* sign over our buffet.

TRAINHOPPER

There is a ferret inside his shirt the whole night.
Tiny ferret claws grip tight to his chest hairs, a furry
bottom nestles in his palm. Every so often, he plops
a bottle of cow milk into the sick creature's mouth
and takes a swig of whisky.

The ferret dies the very next day but that night
he is more popular than the stubborn piñata
or the girls spinning fire with slicked down ponytails.

Trainhopper's stories get louder as the night gnaws on.
He has an oatmeal stout charm. He can tell you
how to skin a raccoon or bottle rattlesnake venom
with such utter delight that you would think he was
the Mr. Rogers of the Anti-Civ Movement.

When he gets to that one about fist fighting those two
scumfucks in the boxcar, I look at my best friend.
It's her thirtieth birthday. Two braids rest on her back.
Eyes gush like fresh Krylon on warm metal. Black
converse, black laces, black jeans rolled at the cuff.
The same two rings she has worn since we were twelve.
She has hitchhiked across the country, ridden a grainer
at sunset, whittled spoons by the fire and now she just
wants to make babies with this man. This man with a sick
ferret in his shirt.

PEP TALK FOR GIRL SINGERS
(especially Penny Hill)

When your heart has slipped from its case,
bounced across the driveway and landed
in the mint green lawn chair.

When the van is broken down and the venue
cancelled and you are so tired of plucking;
it seems no one wants to hear another
damn girl song. Some ragamuffin coffee
shop singer with a pretty scarf for a guitar strap.
You are thinking of getting implants.
Changing your name to Missy Obvious
so you can at least sell some damn records
to all these vinyl breasts bouncing, heads
bobbing to skin/grunt/slap. At least then,
you would feel like you are moving something.

On those days, I say, go stand in the yard.
With your dirty petticoat and kazoo and sing
nonsense to the sky until the clouds move.
You let them be black light and shake shake.
You be kite string and hillside, cabin and refuge,
acres of what Becoming sounds like.
You be our one woman search party with
a thousand flood lights shining on anything
that looks like truth. Don't you dare think
that the truth is ever unoriginal. There
is no expiration date on your purpose.
Your talent can not be revoked. The Universe
never runs out. Girl, we will never stop
needing you to sing about it.

SARAH

Some girls collect stiff dolls or teacups or acrobatic hearts.
She collects boats. Lines them neat along her crooked shore.
Strokes their metal bellies, their sturdy spines. Nibbles loose
their salty paint. Each boat is named for something lost.

Recess. Soft Blanket. Good Morning. Lassie the Fish. Greg.

She has never taken them out on the water. She is horrified
by whales. She instead, sits by their side. Waxes their necks.
Lullabies their empty bows with the sweaty crest and trough
of her breath. Last night, she fell asleep in the hull, dreamed

of an injured tsunami. Today, she knows how to love them.

She will gather twine and cable. Gather wrench and ratchet.
Snap planks, rip sails, smash open their use. Paste shoulder
blades together with sap and brine. Construct a night-sized
sculpture from their ruin. They will never, ever leave her.

HAPPINESS IS A HOT MESS

There are vegetables overflowing from every surface,
growing from pots, saved from dumpsters: crooked
sculptures in bowls. The windows are open. Sampson
and Delilah are necking, frenzied black fur and growl.

Lemon Engine is learning the banjo. Cigarette perched
on bottom lip, clumsy claw hammer. Occasionally, she
looks up to see if she is disturbing anyone. Even
the ceramic owls are tapping their feet. The ants two-
step along mean trails of cayenne. No one is going
anywhere.

The shower curtain keeps falling. The door is off its
hinges. This house is not used to such warm sirens.
Rising up smells like lavender oil and a pile of sweaty
girls. I fell off my bike yesterday. I've been admiring
the wound all morning.

Abundance is a handmade grail, filled with mulberry
mead. All these years, I had mistaken it for a clean
house and a full bank account. When it came, I didn't
even notice the casual spill. How it stained the linens.
Made every crevice glow so loud and sweet.

SEED CLEANERS

"Everyone in me is a bird.
I am beating all my wings.
They wanted to cut you out
but they will not."

— Anne Sexton, "In Celebration of My Uterus"

BOSTON MARRIAGE

My mother says *every straight girl has an
Anne Heche Moment*. Where they meet
a woman so amazing they question
everything about their sexuality. My
mother's Anne Heche Moment was
named Kate. We think this is how my
sister really got her name. While pregnant,
the doctors told her it was a boy. She cried
so hard, she gave birth to a girl. There are
no fathers in my family. Only men who
marry mothers. Men who leave mothers.
Sometimes I think if a man could hold
me hard enough it would make my
grandmother feel wanted. When I told
my mother I was engaged to a black
man, she said *It's just... so hard.* Her throat
pinched between finger and thumb of
1968; glass bottles thrown at her head.
Students rioting in the street, shouting
her name. I said, *Mama, people don't act like
that anymore.* After the divorce, they told
me the only way a woman in Oklahoma
could lose custody of her kids was if she
was a murderer or gay. The first time I
made love to a woman, we felt like two
wooden matches with one eager head. An
elegant factory mistake. My grandmother
said they used to call lesbian couples
Boston Marriages. The first time I fell in
love with a woman I held her fist in my
palm for hours. How strange that I could
not make a baby with this swelling seed.
When I held my lover in the capitol
rotunda as they declared marriage to be
for one man and one woman. I wish I had
kissed her mouth so loud we shattered
the cacophony of hymns and protests but
I stayed silent. I stayed silent.

Dear Lauren Barry

Right now, you are terrified of stopping suddenly, large rats, and being alone. The rat thing won't go away but the other two will. Right now you like to sleep until noon and watch 90210 reruns. You won't believe this but in a few years you will love disgusting things like artichokes and dark beer. You will suddenly hate strawberry milk and pancakes. When you roll up to work bumping N.P.R. you will smirk at how grown you've become. But girl, this grown ass woman business is no joke.

I want to tell you to go to college but only because for the next ten years you will fantasize about what it would have been like to have nothing else to do but learn. Like when you haven't slept in days. When the baby won't let you close the shower curtain. When you are mopping an entire jar of honey from the kitchen floor. When you finally get the courage to leave him and you do not know how you will survive. You will stare at the blurry scene of cut-off notices, dried pudding cups, heaps of laundry, and you will imagine what it would have been like to hop trains or go to college in Brazil like your friends did. But the truth is you still have nothing else to do but learn.

You will learn that your intelligence does not need a certificate to declare itself useful. You will learn that you are useful. You can check homework; unclog the sink and alphabet rhyme at the same time. You will teach your son how to pee standing up and your daughter how to receive compliments. They will teach themselves how to ride bikes and swim in the deep end. They will teach you how to let go.

When the marriage ends you will not go back to your maiden name. You will not care how they pronounce it, just so long as they know there are some things you never give back. The hardest decision you will ever make will not be to keep the baby, get the divorce, or let yourself fall in love with a girl, it will be quitting your job to become a poet. You will have nightmares about your children sitting on the curb with flies buzzing around them. I want to tell you this won't happen. But the truth is, I still don't know. I have no idea if you are going to make it but here's the thing, Lauren, one day, you will be performing poetry at a women's shelter and a nineteen-year-old girl will come up to you covered in bruises and tears. She is terrified of stopping suddenly, large rats, and being alone.

LINEAGE

My mom was in the first punk rock band in Oklahoma City.
Dead Bloated Carp. Eventually they changed their name to
Whores of Babylon. The only gigs they could get were strip
clubs. My mom's job was to get patrons to pay attention to them.
Luckily, she was a fishnet fox. Think Cindy Lauper meets
Greta Garbo. She played that tambourine like
she was shaking the juice from a devoured peach.

My grandmother married her first husband after he got her
pregnant. She was the prettiest prude girl on campus.
He bet his best friend his brand new Fender Stratocaster
that he could get her in the sack. He got to keep his guitar
and fifty-five years later, as the president of the Arkansas
chapter of Right to Life, he tells me if Roe V. Wade
had happened before The Bet, my mother would not
have been born.

My great-grandmother waited tables at age fourteen. Saved
all the money that didn't go to feeding her siblings to buy
a pair of the new transparent leg-shaped stockings. She was
never allowed to go anywhere but work or church. One night,
her flaming brother powdered her face white as a movie actress
and sent her out on the town. She came home with the words
Indian Whore burned into her thighs.

2007

Our fathers both
died that year.
Their rusty organs
collapsed under the
weight of escape.

The house burned
bright that year—
I watched from
across the street.
Held a baby
in a blanket
while you held
your new guitar.

I kissed another
man that year.
Dreamed him up,
big as sirens.
Climbed out of
myself to reach
his wax lips.

The ice storm
screamed that year.
Thick shards fell,
severed our flimsy
veins. Our fingers
were so stiff
we could not
find each other
in the dark.

SMALL ENOUGH TO FIT

If you were small enough to fit
on a bite of mashed potatoes,
would you go up or down?
What does September mean?
I am seven in September.
When are we all going to get
married again? I dance good
at the marriage. I look cool
when I dance. If I was as big
as a dragon, I could really do
the caterpillar. It would mess
the ground up though. This is
my dragon. It breathes frosting
and has octopus feet. It's only
alive in the winter. It drinks Coke
for power. I can't drink Coke
because my mom doesn't
let me, plus it tastes like bomb juice.
Why do we keep having to go to
school? I don't learn anything
there. I just eat burritos and sing
about letters. Well, I learned how
to make a square with my fingers.
I know how to spell I and Like
and You. I like you. I like you.
I like you. I like you. I like my
cat. He has one eye and he's a
boy. Everyone else is a girl.
I like to rap about my cat.
The morning is the best time
to rap. You can hear yourself
in your brain when you rap.
How do ears make sound?
Can I turn my eyes backward
so I can see the strings of blood
in there? In the old days, did we

wear shirts? In the old days,
did we have tongues?

Stormchaser
(for Kait)

As my sister rode away in the back seat of a cop car,
a dragon finally caught, fire leaking from her eyelids,
wings pinned behind her. I picked up everything she owned
scattered across the sidewalk in front of the bar and
placed back in her only home, a yellow, velvet-lined
guitar case with no guitar.

The living room contained a dented can of black beans,
three different Converses and A+ homework wadded up
in rubber bands. The bedroom contained an extra sock
and three extra shirts that smelled like highways, blisters,
and roach clips. Tucked in the little nook off the den
was a luggage tag with her dead father's name on it and
a note I had written her ten years ago that said:

Kait, don't forget to feed the cats. Mom will.
They'll blame you. I love you. Don't go in my room.

My sister's home was a womb built from a one-night stand
turned straight jacket. The other tenants screamed so loud
she had to bang her foot on the ceiling to get some sleep.
She moved out at 7 a.m. on a Monday morning. Ready to go
to work. An Aries born in a house of Aquarians. A match
born in a glass of water. Always trying to spark but just
blowing a fuse with the effort.

At eight years old, she refused to play with Barbies,
but constructed entire cities for them, complete with
cardboard libraries and dryer lint storm clouds. This is
when we knew there was something kind of different
about her. It wasn't just that her favorite movie was
Twister or that she knew a freaky amount of information
about Helen Hunt, it was that she watched the sky.
Like other kids watch for Santa. She was praying for
wall clouds.

She is our own Doppler radar. She feels the shift
of the wind and the trees getting anxious. She runs
screaming on a warm spring day, *The twister is coming
y'all! The twister is coming.* When the meteorologist
finally issues a warning and we all take cover, she runs
toward it. If she could just hop in that pick-up truck
spinning in its eye and be flung back to
a planet where we have cumulus hearts that pour out
love without judgment on anything willing to receive.
Around here, we prefer drunk to perceptive and Kait can
hear corruption in fruit seeds. She hears cash transactions in
school bells. She drinks to calm the Doppler.

Tonight when she was fighting the police officer, her mouth
a goblet of a hurricanes, I wanted to tell her

Kait, not every storm is worth chasing. Sometimes you
have to take shelter. Build the house yourself. Let their
answers beat on you like hail on a snare drum but you
just keep thumping out your song. You're the only one
who knows it. You chose this body this life and this
family like we chose you and I promise we'll quit
trying to change you if you'll quit trying to leave us.

When mom asks me for the thousandth time, What are
we supposed to do with her? I'll say, Let's build her a
telescope so she can watch the stratospheres squabble.
Let's find her guitar so she can make music when the
Doppler gets too loud. Let's paint her walls with pink
lightning and hold her tight. Until she knows that all
that fire is not for burning things down. It's for giving
us the brightest light.

ALL THE NOISE

The flies dropped fast from the vodka fumes. Speckled
the carpet with their drunken wings. Stench more like evening
mouth than corpse. His liver still gasping like gills. His
music still crackled and flopped, drenched
the blue dining room.

The daughter walked over to his record player, broke off
the tired arm, sharpened the needle on her teeth, plunged it
just below his lung. Mingus and Coltrane rang through
his spleen. A slight twitch then hum as she dug deeper for the things
she knew belonged to her. A golden locket or ceramic
unicorn, perhaps. Things she knew he would have
given her if he could ever find her house.

She found the hollow cage of a snare drum and two clean
bicycle tires. Then she heard the click click spring of calculator
keys. She pried open his kidney, felt around with her fingers, was stunned

when she found a small, careful woman with a page-boy haircut,
black square glasses. It was Denise.

She had almost forgotten about Denise, his girlfriend of
twenty-four years. The last time, bruised and naked, huddled
against the linen closet. Now here, so miniature, hunched over
her machine, punching numbers. Punching like a soft bass line.
Punching a tally of debts. A quiet settlement offer. Denise
wasn't at all afraid. Not at all resentful. She was just a ledger book,
a gentle accountant.

The daughter decided then and there to give up searching for
what was rightfully hers. She was no longer a lender, instead, an offering.
Just as she began to close the opening she found a birthday card.
On the front, a question, loudly slurred:
Do you want to know the true name of God?
All the Noise,
All the Silence.

SUITCASE OF IMPOSSIBLE

That night we emptied everything.
The twenty-seven-story chocolate cake,
the curly-haired girl who climbs to the top
to place the cherry, a room made of icing,
a music box where the white dwarves keep
the pale blue sky at night, the Cleveland
County tooth fairy who has paid her $8.50,
and the bearded king with reindeer.

It all started when she asked me what *gay*
meant and why her teacher says *gay people
are going to hell* and if I thought kids could
go there.

The only thing worse than coming into contact
with someone who has unthinkably wrong ideas
is finding out that person has been in contact with
your children.

You get to keep anything you want in there,
I said. Some people choose a fiery place to send
bad people when they die. Some choose statues
or beads or elaborate ceremonies. Some
just want a chocolate fountain super slide or
detachable limbs. Some don't want anything.

We went through each item we carry. Holding them
up to the light to see if they still fit. When we got to
Santa Claus, she wept in my arms for ten minutes.

Suddenly, she sat straight up, wiped off her cheeks, dusted
off his red velvet sleeves, placed him in her suitcase and said,
I'm keeping him.

GREATEST FEAR

The children whose clothes don't fit
sit on the curb, wait for their mother.
She never comes. They grow hungry.
Their ankles are cold. Hot dogs roast
in backyards. They walk toward home.
Cut their toes on pebbles. Strangers
ask if they want candy. Snatch them
with dirty fists. Throw them in wide
velour backseats.

The children whose clothes don't fit
scream so loud the fire hydrants release.
Streets flood. Gold statues of families
drown like patio furniture. Potted plants.
Wet flags.

The children whose clothes don't fit
grab hold of a casserole-shaped raft.
Their wounds smoothed by salty panic.
They float up on the shore of their lawn.
Their mother has slept through it all.
Aspartame drains from her wrists,
diet soda cans spill out the door.

She is awake now. A granite tomb
in the sunshine. She knits them wool
socks. The children feel safe at home.

MENAGE À WILDERNESS

*"I saw the open eye of night, all
guileless, all iris of a starshine grey,
scattered with clusters of brilliant pupils."*

—Sharon Olds, "Wilderness"

Dear Lemon Engine II

If I only had five pairs of socks, all the same color. If I drank a gallon of water and went on a walk every day. If I got rid of everything that didn't make me gush with giddy. If I became an herbivore. If I only had to work three hours a day. If I cried more and thought less. If I could just talk to you every time I want to sort things out. This would be a telephone wire and we would be birds, the most hilarious birds. We would send shudders of laughter all the way to Maine.

You haven't spoken to me in days. A dozen girls dressed in black are at my house to shoot a music video. The fire ants are in my room. I can't even go home. I didn't know it would go like this. Remember that one night? Tangled on the living room floor in front of the window? The sky was a disco. You took me on a scavenger hunt for your crazy. I found nothing but peach pits and crushed eggshells, the kinds of things that bloom into the brightest yellow. If you played me a song for every mistake you ever made, I would never stop turning the tape over. Our ex-lovers are a supper bowl of dandelion heads and red bud flowers. We found them in the wild. Loved them hard. Let them go. We always let them go.

We just have too much lightning crammed into our hearts. Just want someone to put her ear to our chest and tell us how far away the storm is.

Holy Mother of Blisters, I miss you.

TALLY OF QUEERDOM
{IN NO PARTICULAR ORDER}

4.
She lifts her suit trousers to reveal her rainbow socks.
Little sparkly letters spell out *My Lucky Socks*.
Quick sexy squint, sideways smirk. She is a bent light beam
in a grey cubicle farm. I will go home with her tonight.

11.
I am a whisky julep. Spread sweaty on the floor.
I've lost an earring. Sore hips. I am some shade of marmalade.
There is melted sunset all over the carpet. I have never spilled
in this shape before. She licks the inside of my ankle. Tells me
it tastes like peaches.

2.
The back porch is washed in the milk paint of moonlight.
The garden is showing off its unruly curves. Teasing me
with twelve shades of green and the sweet scent of curry.
I am alone with my body. More turned on than I can recall.
The highway behind the house shouts as loud as my veins.
I stroke the wisteria. Whisper *What have you done to me?*

8.
We take turns giggling. Shifting from femme bones to
boy bones. Quiet maneuvering through the landscape
of energies. Identity is a swing. We are straddled like spiders.

13.
She tells the catfish story to the redneck like she is sliding
a hook through his fat, watering mouth. Unlike his story
of the prize-winning Monster Blue, hers ends with a stringer
full of fish corpses, eaten alive by raccoons. I like her story.
Mostly I like how his face changed from salesman to friend
as soon as she dropped the trotline. Also, I like to imagine her
perched easy on red sandstone, speaking release to the shore.

7.

In the kitchen, she presses me against the counter and kisses
me madly. Her brother's wife saunters in to refresh her mint
julep and gasps. Fumbles, awkward, back to the living room.
Later, she confides, her husband has never kissed her so deeply.
She has never been caught in the act. We all have different ways
of fastening our sex shut. Slipping a nametag in our underwire.
Zipping up our strange beneath our pin striped trousers.

12.

I am more terrified of monogamy/commitment/entrapment than
I am of lesbian/bisexual/wild woman/queer. Wedding rings look
like handcuffs. I do not want a circle drive or master bedroom.
I don't care what the neighbors think. I tackle her on the couch
just before the L-word snags my cheek. She knows how easy it is
for a poet to get all tangled in the reel. Instead, she says *applesauce*.
Asks me to be her *jellyfish*. I lick her accountant ears. Tell her they
taste like good sense.

1.

I am thirteen. On the bus headed to church camp. My first boyfriend
nervously asks me if I would ever kiss a girl. I explain my clumsy
theory of the spectrum for the first time. How we are shades
of masculine and feminine. How I kiss beings, not genders or races
or wallets. Sixteen years later, he tells me the night before that bus
ride, he kissed his best friend, Greg. He never told anyone. He called
just to thank me for that.

Jealousy Is a Mean Beach

I am the heirloom tomato
on the Betty Boop towel.
You've forgotten my name.
You always say things like,
I am in love with your mind
but there are no minds here.
There are Crisco-covered
mounds of flesh.
Bikini-clad dreamsicles,
slow-motion running.
Supple drumsticks basting
in the sun. I have a mouth
full of jellyfish. Stinging lips
get smacked with a volleyball.
Sharks are scared of this beach.
The crustaceans have all
had work done. No one
can live here. Jagged shore
gashes feet. They place a conch
shell to my ear, tell me *Listen
for your lost love.* Tease my
freckled heart. Poke my mushy
ribs. I just want you to love me
like I own you.

SWEETHEART

When I introduced you as my sweetheart,
you called it *convenient*. Noted how easy it was
to hold your hand on Gay Day, in a room full
of Andrea Gibson fans but how I couldn't kiss
you in the hallway at work.
There are a million kinds of bravery.
I only have the Talking to Large Groups kind down.
I am a flimsy fist. A shallow protest.
You wore a tux with heels to the inaugural ball.
I want to be you when I grow up.

You asked me what the hell *sweetheart* means.

It means you are the only person I allow to pee
while I am brushing my teeth. The only person
I can sleep wrapped in. You understand my need
for climate control. How reading aloud is the best
foreplay ever. I think it's sexy when you correct
my grammar. My grandmother says she's so grateful
you're pretty. The word *Poly* makes you cringe.
The word *Commitment* makes me twitch.
I called you my *This Friend*. You roll your eyes.
You feel like you are on a baited hook.
You use fishing metaphors more than I do.
I feel like we are a balanced teeter-totter.
I can't wink or play pinball for shit.
Your Galaga skills put large nerds to shame.
You are the Pleasure Empress. You are coozies
and an ice-cold beer purse. You play games like darts
and dominoes and things I consider to have too much
math in them. I only have three jokes and they all
involve condiments. You tell jokes in other languages.
You collect geological porn and inside joke tee shirts.
I collect chapbooks and Buddhas.
You have an amusement park for a sock drawer.
I never wear any. When you are stressed I can see it

in your neck. When I am stressed I locate your elbow
and call it home.

Maybe sweetheart is a fanny pack kind of word.
Maybe it is an expired parking meter. Maybe all
the other words broke down when they reached us.
We should panhandle for new words.

*It was never
about the word*, you say.

There is a closet on every
corner. Some doors stick a little.

Sweetheart, today I am wearing nothing
but your ninja socks.

DEAR POET

Stop fucking shit up.

I know words are the sail of your bones.
I know you are black-capped painter,
artiste extraordinaire.

But if I say I was carrying a crate of bananas
down the apartment steps,
do not say they were grapefruits,
do not say they were her steps,
do not say they were the size of her breasts,
because the only she that will read this
does not have steps,
does not have grapefruit breasts,
instead has perfect cups of caramel,
instead has a house with a yard,
she will wonder why you were carrying breasts
down some girl's steps. It will be uncomfortable.

Dear Poet,
you are the noisiest highway.
You like the sound of curtains slapping,
words like *banjo sweat* and *love blisters*.
You want someone to tell everything to
even though everything is never accurate.
She won't understand. Or she will understand.
Seven times, she will understand.
I will tell her it was The Poet,
I will say Baby, I am sorry I was never
in a juniper tree with a warm canary.
I was never longing for a girl named
Lemon Engine, it was The Poet that
needed the sounds to cream at the top.

Dear Poet,
if you fuck things up with her this time, I swear
I will not let you smell her hibiscus hair.

Nor count the blackbirds perched on the stoplight.
Damnit, I will not even let you hold her in her ocean room.
It is not even a fucking ocean room, it is just painted blue.
You will not rest on the raft in the wake of the tidal wave.
Will not mountain turtle, nor peach marmalade. You will
be left in a mall food court and forced to text the dude
who replaces every S with Z and never gets it
when you replace their name with Truck Stop.

HOW TO STAY CELIBATE

Write lots of poems about sex. Hang them in your closet
like skinny jeans. Fantasize about the moment you can finally
slip into them.

Go on dates with men who drive Escalades. Who call you *Shorty*
and grin sideways as *Lil' Freak* bangs through the speakers.

Plant the basil without a shovel. Hold the dirt in your fingers until
your mouth waters.

Practice your wink. Perfect your cuddle.

Brush up against the woman in the sea-foam dress,
allow your chest to coo.

Swallow your tea carefully. Watch the sunset recklessly.

Sing prayers into your orange kazoo.

Cancel the picnic, show up late, barely miss him each time.

Cook purple potato soup, drink wine at a table full of windmills.
Let their breeze give you all the energy you need.

Go on long walks with yourself.

Pack up all your pronouns and preferences; sell them in the yard sale.
People will buy anything.

Listen to a goddess play banjo to the tomato plants.

Let him hug you a little too long.

Climb the juniper tree with a stranger.

Steal bricks from demolished condominiums. Trim the womb-
     shaped garden
with the rubble of the fortunate.

Learn the fine art of making stew. Serve it to hungry people.

Learn the fine art of making out. Practice with hungry people.

Type all letters to lovers backwards so they must look in the mirror when they want to be close to you.

Give up the need to finish things. Knit one sock.

GORGEOUS BEASTS

They say it's only one step away from bestiality.
Pretty soon, we'll be screwin' goats and dawgs.
Maybe some chickens, if we can get
a hold of dem purdy necks.

We pour out our best drawl. Thick
and stout against the glass of our
sickened pits. We laugh with big,
deliberate, serrated teeth.
The knife goes in clean.

When we have swallowed
the last of the rowdy, each
couple cakewalks to
their bedroom.

The one-eyed boy kitten
nuzzles up to the black boy
dog and nurses on his stiff
nipples.

When we moan and growl
and toss each other around
on the mattress, the animals
think we are playing.
They scurry over to offer a paw,
a rough tongue. We push them
away. Tell them,
Be careful, pretty soon
you'll be screwin' humans,
and we all know how
disgusting
that is.

Dear Lemon Engine III

I have been scrubbing and painting the kitchen for three days now. When I get tired, I imagine you coming home from your tour and lighting up at the sight of it. You will take all the vegetables out of the fridge. We'll slice them up for your famous curry as you tell me stories about the road. I imagine there will be stories of sweet girl lips, drunken frat boys talking over the music. I will show you how I organized the spices by region of the world and ask *Why on earth do we have so much cardamom and coriander?* You'll explain the difference between java cardamom and bastard cardamom. We will laugh hysterically at the idea of bastard cardamom as you start the teakettle.

Remember that day when you and Drea were cooking in the kitchen and I was coloring with the kids? I think it was Easter. It hadn't rained in forty days and it was finally pouring outside. Drea was complaining of a headache and you said *Maybe it's the radiation. I mean it hasn't rained since the tsunami and all that radiation from the nuclear plant has just been sitting in the ocean and now it's raining on us.* We laughed about the absurdity of such a thing but I could tell you were serious.

When that crazy old man said the world would end we sat around drinking beers and talking about what we would do if it really were our last night. Everyone talked about the food they would eat and the sex they would have. Your eyes went frantic as you talked about how it could always be your last night and what a relief it would be if you had some certainty about it. Like how much peace you'd have instead of the constant uncontrollable threat. I wanted to hold you against my chest and tell you all that Buddhist mumbo jumbo about there being no permanence in form but instead I brought you another beer from the fridge. Right now, I feel how you must feel all the time.

Sam shot himself yesterday. My brother's best friend. He lived with us for a while when we were teenagers. I just keep thinking about his brain. He did so many drugs for so long it was like he shattered into a thousand Sams. What if I have no idea who is talking inside me?

At the wake, we were packed into the blistering hot living room, crying and sweating. Pouring out all the voices until there was just a puddle of broken glass. I wish you had been there. Everyone clung to their fragile aliveness, you would have felt right at home. When will you ever come home?

Holy Mother of Everything, Grace.

FLATLAND GOSPEL

"But come here, fear
I am alive and you are so afraid
of dying."

— Joy Harjo, "I Give It Back"

WORLD'S TALLEST HILL

In Poteau, Oklahoma there stands a hill, one foot shy
of being a mountain. 1,999 feet of boasting pride
all the way to the top.

At the top of the hill, shiny trucks line up like churches.
Giddy swarms of sixteen-year-old mothers out late
on a Friday night. Frosted lips and too much eyeliner.
Boys in sagging shorts and big cowboy buckles.
Ice chests full of six-point beer purchased just over
the state line. There is a chrome-and-bass boxing
match. Tinted windows shaking like bedposts.
Turn it up ya'll, this is my jam.
This is weekend medicine.
Billy just got his ink done. It grips tight to his bicep
like Carla, who can't stand the way Brandy be lookin' at him.
Shit's about to get rowdy tonight.

Right now, you can look out over the hill
and see the twenty-four-hour Wal-Mart glowing
like the queen bee in the hive.
A steady stream of headlights loop around
from Wal-Mart to the movie theater and back again.

This how we learn how to move in circles.
How to move in packs.

You can look out over that hill and see Liz.
Tough smirk of a girl. Playing basketball
in the First Baptist parking lot.
Her palms pound so hard they are as calloused
as a dude's. She likes to be called *Dude*.
Dude will show up at Prom in a tux and leave
with cheeks bloody as corsage.

This is how we learn how to break each other down.

Over at the drive-thru, Daniel is working
the closing shift. Saving up to get the hell out of here.

Hair perfectly spiked over his visor. Uniform collar popped.
No one comments on his mascara or the touch of concealer.
He is flawless. Brutal wink of a boy. He's been called *fag* so much
he dropped a beat behind it and made it his ring tone.

This is how we learn how to man up.

Rachel works on cars with her dad in the garage.
Glenn Beck rattles through the speakers like engine grease.
Rachel has been in love with a girl for two years but she believes
in family values. She knows with all her heart she is going to hell
if she doesn't straighten up.

This is how we get control. How we fit in. How we stay small town
in a scary world.

Mr. Elgin shoots BB guns at black boys for getting white girls pregnant.
Michael climbed to the top of a cell phone tower to get some attention.
Beth eats Xanax by the fistful. Jamie built a meth-lab in her sparkly bedroom.
Jenny herds cattle by day, strips at night.

This is how we learn how to cope.

This is how we build pride
one foot shy of a mountain.

GLOSSOLALIA

EE Shunda-lo Mo-kai
He remembers the fit.
The way the Spirit fell.
Tumbled and stomped
in her cheeks, spilled
out like a crate of ripe
plums. Vera was old,
caught the same spirit
every Sunday night.
He was five and still
remembers each
fleshy syllable.
How they waited
to see who would
catch the meaning.
How the storefront
church hollered and
shook with magic.
He knew even then
that the holy ghost
was only for adults.
If he were to scream,
flail about in the aisles,
they'd think the demons
had him.
Hold him down, deep
into the night until
they could pierce
the evil, hook the black
flopping scales and rip it
from his fragile soul.
He began to pray
not to the heavens,
not to his preacher father,
but to the Glorious Spectacle
for a sharp stone tongue.

To the Oklahoma Lawmakers Who Passed SB 1878 Requiring Women to Receive an Ultrasound Prior to an Abortion

Why don't you print out the ultrasound pictures
and pastel frame them? Make me take them home
and hang them on my wall as a souvenir of the night
that is branded like red coals to flesh on my memory.

The night when his hand pressed so hard against
my shoulder blade, I felt more intimacy with asphalt.
Why don't you knit the baby a sweater? Make me
take it out and smell it on the anniversary of this day
for the rest of my life to remind me I chose to be
a murderer instead of bringing a child into a world
where we kill people in the name of freedom,
but imprison people in the name of life.

You could pass laws for that too.
I can still see his handprints on my thighs.
Now I can see your probing eye scraping across
my cervix, tattooing my womb with shame.
Why don't you send me a card every Mother's Day
to remind me of how wretched I am,
sign it, *Your friends at the State Capitol,*
making sure you know we actually do
something all day with your tax dollars.
Look: I know it can get boring, between the Porkers'
Association Breakfast and the Oil and Gas Industry lunch.
I know you need something to do between cutting funding
for the arts and passing off your racism as an immigration
bill, but I need a little more from you than a piece of paper.
I mean, if you really want to show me that you believe in
Faith, Family, and Freedom, then why don't you come along
for the ride? I could have used you that night.

After the football game, he finally shows me attention.
I grasp for acceptance. Tell me I'm special,
so when he hands me the next drink I don't
look to the bottom of it for approval. Tell me to scream
louder so someone might find us. Wrap me in a blanket
when he's done, take me home, my body a tapped keg,
my heart the grimy gym floor after the pep rally.
Give me the words to say to my parents when I come out
of the bathroom with a plus sign on the stick and he won't
even talk to me.

The school hallway is a canyon. Silence echoes in my skull.
I don't know what to do. Tell me what to do.
Sit with me at the clinic, filling out twenty pages
of questions. Make me listen to the heartbeat.
Give me the revelation that the blip on the screen
is actually a baby. Take me home when I change my mind.
Take me to the doctor every month, hold my
hand in the delivery room. I will name him after you
if you will help me do my homework when he's
crying in the next room. Give me food stamps,
pay my gas bills. Put him in an after-school program
where he learns he can sell my pain pills.
Have mercy on him when he goes to court.
Give me strength when they sentence him.
If you want to play God,
Mr. and Mrs. Lawmakers,
if you want to write your Bible
on my organs,
then you better be there
when I am down on my knees
pleading for relief
from your morality.

TARANTISM

*Tarantism - n. A malady characterized by
an uncontrollable urge to dance. Erroneously
believed to result from the bite of a tarantula.*

It started with a little shoulder twitch.
Like shaking flies from their brief perch.
It was subtle. Shiny shoes tapping under
oak desks. Their starched collars rubbed
like maracas against their necks. It was
hard to debate. Hard to vote. Hard to sit
in committee with their knees knocking
against the bench. Soon, they were lined
up in the aisles. Arm in arm, kicking their
wool legs like tambourines. Gold-framed
paintings of old men rattled off the walls.
There were funky chickens and butterflies.
There were stiff elbow jitterbugs. Crooked
hip swing. Cajun two-step. Jackets swirled
and flung. Silver hair whipped madly. Jerky
sprinklers and flopping guppies caught on
saucy reels. Ties became leashes. Rickety
windmills burned into the carpet. Some
kind of electric boogaloo broke out in the
chamber bathroom. No one could escape.
No one knew what was happening.
Suddenly they were drenched in sweat,
delirious with goofy grins. They forgot
all about what they were fighting for.

To the Oklahoma Progressives Plotting Mass Exodus

There is a sick pit in your stomach.
A plantation in your front yard.
The static flicker of black and white.
An absurd talking picture,
where sepia skin is now villain.
You are not sure whom to trust anymore.
Everyone walks backwards in your neighborhood.
You are surrounded by billboards with hate-sized font.
You are looking for a secret handshake.
A fish with feet drawn in the sand.
Blue paint on the doorframe.
You resent even the dirt for being so damn red.
At night you are a furious search engine.
Screaming down the track toward
some kind of Shangri-La.
Portland has no jobs.
Canada doesn't want you.
You hear property is cheap in Costa Rica.
Even Egypt seems safer than your next PTA meeting.
Anywhere is better than here.

But here is your home.

Here is where you chose to raise your kids,
because the people are so friendly.
Do not let them drive you away.

Here is where the sunset stretches its arms wide as forgiveness across
　　stolen plains.
Here is where Clara Luper sat down at the Katz lunch counter and
　　started the sit-in movement.
Here is where black and white soldiers fought alongside each other
　　for the first time.
Where Kate Barnard was elected to office before she had the right to vote.
Here is where Charlie Christian learned guitar.

Where Wayne Coyne keeps the bubble.
Where Woody Guthrie played the harmonica for sandwiches.
Here is the land of the heart.
It's where the healing has to take place.
Tell them you are not moving.
Oklahoma is worth the wait.

Sometimes evolution feels like
the stinging cramp in the back of your knees
when you grow too fast for your bones.
Sometimes it feels like a house in the city
with three goats, ten chickens, and twelve anarchists.

Tear up the sidewalk.
Plant a garden.
Bake a squash casserole and invite
all your terrified neighbors over.
Say *A Salaam Alaikum* to everyone you meet.
Fill out all government forms in Español.
Check all the boxes for your race.
Ride your bike to work.
Make art in the streets.
Feed people without a license.
Go to city council meetings.
Sit in at the State House and Senate.
Wear a purple boa.
Do not apologize for your presence.
Write love letters to mothers and fathers in prison.
To the wardens, the police officers, the judges.
Write love letters to queer kids and their bullies.
Tell them you are staying here for THEM.
Kiss a republican on the cheek.
Show them how to love someone you don't understand.
DO SOMETHING with that tight fist.
That broken heart.
That liberal mouth.
Progress is a series
of small bold moves.
Don't leave.

Here is where
we need you.

THE PRAYER MERCHANT

This town is dusty shelves and the traffic of pigeons.
I knew he wouldn't stay long. Awkward hanger of a man.
Faded pin stripes and wing-tipped shoes. Said he'd make
me a real nice deal. So many small boxes. Spread out

like his staircase grin. He placed the pink, careful one in my palm.
I told him I was not a sweet-skirt genuflect. I prefer unraveled hymns.
The rumble of cloud against field. I fingered the edges

of the moon box. It felt like the slow wane and drift of my father.
The merchant said it would go with my eyes but *far away* is a color
I wear too often. He asked what a pretty girl like me could possibly
need. I need my prayers close. Urgent as

mattress. Sturdy as femur. Canoe-shaped and racing toward *Holy Shit.*
My bones have no need for wishes. They yearn to be telescopes.
Do you have any broken ones? A rusty swing set? A clarinet with
chipped reed? Where are the sounds

we almost miss? Heaven is a tight fist that never blooms. The people
here are made of petals.

WOMEN BEHIND BARS

I was six months pregnant, pushing
a Cheerio-munching toddler in the grocery cart.
We stopped by the photo lab to pick up our Christmas
pictures and kept shopping. It was a lot of lentils
back in those days. Rice and ramen noodles.
I spent forty-two dollars on the week's groceries and left the store.
On the way out the security guard stops me, asks
if he can look in my diaper bag, pulls out the pictures
I forgot to pay for.
I apologize profusely, offer to pay for them.
He chuckles his eight-dollar-an-hour chuckle and
says *You had the chance to pay for them, lady.*
Escorts me to the camera room. Groceries left
outside, baby girl on hip, I notice myself on the
TV monitor, wearing my favorite denim maternity
shirt and cropped pants.

I am startled by how responsible I look.

You might want to call someone to pick up your kid.
I would hate for Child Services to take her.

No, you don't understand. I cannot
go to jail, I don't do that anymore.

When my mom gets there to pick up my daughter,
the cop arrives and it's a woman. I think maybe she
will have some sympathy but she just tells me to watch
my belly as she puts me in the cop car. Says she won't
handcuff me in front of my daughter if I don't start acting
crazy. By the time I'm checked into county, I am hunched
over from the exhaustion of weeping. A woman my age
sits down next to me.

Honey child, you don't need to be worrying like that.
All that stress is gonna upset the baby.

Her name is Sylvia, she has two gold teeth,
a sparkle in her eye, and the sweetest giggle when she
talks about the food in this place. I won't tell her this
is the third time I've been here, that I know how bad
the food tastes. I want her to think that I don't belong here.
I used to steal stuff when I was a kid.
I used to sell cocaine in the girls' bathroom.
I thought that if I could just get high enough,
it would make the pain float away.

This story is not pain.

I am white.
I am three times less likely to be incarcerated
than a black woman.
But let's say for a second that I'm not.
That my grandpa is not an attorney.
That the charges weren't dropped.

Let's say,
I'm Sylvia.
I grew up on the east side.
I used to have a good job
making ten dollars an hour at a factory.
Then the factory moved to Thailand
where they will work for two dollars.
So, I started selling weed while
I looked for work, 'cause I never been
one to beg for money. It's not like weed
ever hurt nobody, not like cocaine. I'm just
headed to the grocery store, baby girl in the back seat.
I ain't picking up no Christmas pictures.
I can barely afford these diapers.
My headlight's out. My tag's expired.
The cop pulls me over. I can't afford an attorney.
Who's gonna watch my baby?
My mama hates me because my stepdad liked me better.
My baby's daddy only calls when he's drunk.
I'm trying to do right. I go to church. I've been saved
three times but who is saving me now?

I am your evening entertainment.
Declare me wrong.
Declare me unfit.
Declare me Not You.
The more you are afraid of me,
the easier it is to
sell you a multi-billion-dollar industry.
Tell yourself, I am danger
when really I'm just cheap labor.
See now I'm finally working again.
Workin' for the state for twenty-two cents an hour.

Funny how well our system works.

For every hundred thousand women in Oklahoma,
one hundred and twenty-four are incarcerated. The national average
    is seventy-five.
Massachusetts clocks in at eleven. Someone will profit
as this number increases. The rest of us
will just keep shopping.

AFTER THE REV

We might need these after the rev, she says.
Clenching an orange plastic bottle with little blue tablets
that she found behind the dumpster. The name Gertrude
typed out on the prescription label.

No, she is not Gertrude.
Yes, she is wearing roller skates.
Yes, she has a satchel full of persimmon cookies
because the city is full of persimmons this year.

No, I am not her grandfather who looks at her like she stole
his last name and spray painted it on the side of a ruined building
No, I am not her mother, who mumbles after dinner
What a shame. All that private school tuition gone to waste.
Yes, I wonder what she means when she says *after the rev.*

Jason screens movies on the side of abandoned churches
to let people in the neighborhood know what the gas company is up to.
Trish is learning how to can. How to use fifty pounds of pears from
     her rent house yard.
Shaneeka likes country music and hunting. She made a prom dress
     from a deer hide.
At East Central High, Mr. Stephens holds a moment of silence for
     the victims
of bullying. It pisses all the parents off. He does it anyway.
Sarah stares at traffic like a bee that no longer recognizes her own hive.
Luis is nineteen and homeless, until he finds a tent in a downtown
     park and
a family of people who glow with what it means to be fed up.

Yes, Luis is a poet.
No, he is not published on some stark page.
Yes, he wrote the poem you heard when you were begging the
     madness to uncloak you.
Yes, he will hug you until it is uncomfortable.
No, he is not insured.
No, we do not know the cause of his death.

They want to know why there is no cohesive message, want
to know why we don't have a slogan, a brand, an identity.
They want you to think that this is just the way it should be.
There is nothing you can do to change it. They want us to
call each other names until we are defeated by our own bullhorn.

No, you cannot fit us neatly on a billboard.
No, there is no party loud enough to claim all of our voices.
Yes, the rev is already happening.
Yes, it is a cloud of pepper spray. A swarm of peaceful fists.
Steady rivers of new information.
Yes, it is also everyday people. Building a mountain of small things.
Choosing to behave strangely instead of blindly.
Yes, it is a room full of shift.
Shouting louder than any bank account.
Listen.
MIC CHECK.
Every day we prepare.
Every day we make some bold move.
Dismantle some lonely treadmill.
Love some unlikely person.
Save something for later.
Learn a new skill.
Depend on them less.
Depend on us more.
Organize a tidal wave.
Until there is no them.
There is only
us.

TRY SURRENDER.
SEE WHAT HAPPENS.

"It is true that your mind is sometimes like a battering ram, running all through the city, shouting so madly inside and out about the ten thousand things that do not matter."

— Hafiz, "Out of the Mouth of A Thousand Birds"

BENEDICTION FOR HUSTLERS AND GARDENERS

When you were 18, you thought you'd be famous before you were 21.
You won all the seed spitting contests.
Carried matchsticks and strobe lights in your briefcase.
Everywhere you went, you were like *Dude! Check this out!*
We were all pretty sure, you were going to be the hottest thing since
Dr. Dre or pomegranate juice.
We'd see you float up to the spot in your platinum canoe and scribble
autographs on the curling bark of willing girls.

You're 27 now, still music out of your trunk.
You're 31 now, still punching clocks in the thick noon of the day.
You're 42 now, still hoping for lava to pour out of traffic lights.

You're too old for all this, you say, after three graveyard shifts
at the Light Bulb Farm, followed by 8 a.m. at the Grown Up Factory.
You used all your vacation time, scattering megaphones along the highway,
and sleeping on crusty motel beds in Iowa.
You wear your business plan on a chain around your neck and call it
    grown folk's bling.
Some days it feels like you are too tall for these carnival rides. All
    their sick flash and cat calls.
It would be so much easier if you could just wear Hawaiian shirts to
    work on Friday and
get giddy about good lumbar support and ergonomic arm rests.
You could trade in your chrome-rimmed tractor for a steady pension
    and call it a day.
But deep down you know
this is the only thing you are here to do.
and THIS IS your year. Something is about to happen for you.

But this "quitting five minutes before the miracle" business is a load
    of mule feed.
The miracle is already happening.
The miracle is that you wake up every morning with art in your eardrums,
You compose gorgeous at the gas pump.
Drop mulch in the checkout lane.
You blink with more passion than some people make love with.

This IS your year. The spring is so ripe with your takeover that the
    moon had to get
closer to the earth than it ever has, just to get a whiff of you.
You are a wild windmill, in a field of oilrigs.
You are the only thing that will keep us moving.
You better stay up on that grind, homie. Let that flour billow up and
    dust our cheeks.
Let the ghosts of couches and TVs haunt the music out of you.
Let your throat be a hollow gourd.
Let the seeds you've been spitting all these years
take root and cover the earth with your purpose.
Let your shoulders not give out.
Let the road not tear you down.
Let the exact right people hear you, at the exact right time.
Let the people expect more from our artists.
Let us not settle for cheap plastic and synthetic hooks.
Let your bass kick us in our sleep, wake us in our stomach.
Give us slow food movement with quick wit service.
Let us remember that when one of us creates,
another is created. Let us remember
when one of us quits planting, none of us can be
bloombox.

Prayer for the Public Self

Divine Highway of Honesty, Radical Lover of Flaws, Sacred Janitor.

We are everywhere. Projected on screens. In a hundred conversations all at once.

We watch each other all the time. We feel important all the time. Every facet of our flawed character is amplified in strange electronic gatherings.

We type without thinking. Think without listening. We keep faith in the delete button, the backspace, the run-and-hide feature, but we never feel hidden. Always exposed.

We are a museum with free admission. We are not always the best curators.

Today we turn our exhibit over to you. Show us the balance between loving the stories of our life and being overwhelmed by our own narcissism.

Allow us to share in each other's unique walk without gathering worth from others' opinions.

Let us not get tangled in the web of a never-ending debate, the skewed and bizarre versions of reality.

Wash clean our perceptions. Wipe the lens of our projectors.

Adjust the lighting so we see our friends for their true selves.

Let us learn from the images we create. Let us unite the many voices of our personalities.

Give us awareness of the Grand Movie of Life. Guide us out of our flashy theater for one sacred moment.

Thank you for your silent hallways, your radical forgiveness, your sparkly technology.

And so it is. Amen.

Prayer for the Oooh Shiny

Giant Laser of Grace, Productive Creator of Galaxies, Endless Circle,
I am distracted. Constantly. My mind is a chaotic tangle of loose wires.
I have so much I want to accomplish. So many new things to create,
projects to finish. My intentions are plenty and golden.
The internet, Dear Goddess. This bizarre spinning web is a powerful magnet.
It's on my phone, Lord. My pocket is a will vacuum.
There are screens everywhere I look. I crave every scene and story.
I want to know all the latest jokes. Be friends with all the smartest people.
It feels like everything is moving so fast, a fire hose of things to see.
I have started this prayer six times.
My circuits are heavy with glow.
Lift me from this madness so I can get some work done.
Let me not reach for electronics to fill empty spaces.
Let me see the tasks before me with eager clarity.
Nudge me back when I wander. Uncloak my helplessness.
Remind me of what I am capable of when I focus.
Give me the focus of an ant colony. The industriousness of bees.
Let the hive be my inspiration, not my distraction.
I need a miracle, Sweet Giver.
I need a brain full of your radiant wisdom.
Hands full of your brilliant action.
Thank you for your constant movement,
your unwavering stillness.
And so it is. Amen.

PRAYER FOR THE SNOBBY

Divine Light Telescope, Stardust and Green Grass Maker, Cosmic Lover of Imperfections,

I am being a snob.

I looked harshly at her mullet. I made fun of him for not knowing the minute details of something only I find valuable to know. I judged their bad taste in paint colors. I joked about their Jesus. I come to you, not in shame, I do not think you know the shape of shame, but I come in humility. The kind of humility that casually fashions mountains and oceans.

Let me know that kind of huge grace. That kind of modesty. The quiet smirk of redwood trees. The silent hum of stars.

Release me in this moment from my need to look down on others. Release me from my snobbery. My judgment. My ego's need to make others feel small in order for me to feel shiny. In this moment, give me a kind of humor that takes no one hostage. Let me see others in the kind of gorgeous light you warm the earth with. Let me see all of us as the awkward drums we are. Awkward drums in ugly Christmas sweaters, shining like the most perfect moons.

Thank you for your patience, for good television, for the moments when I see clearly, and as always, for indoor plumbing.

And so it is. Amen.

Everything Is Going to Be Amazing

Put on your knickers, girl. We gonna eat these heavy
decisions for breakfast. Smother 'em in gravy, wash 'em down
with Grown Ass Woman Soda.

We got this. This is the Big Girl Processing Plant.
Don't nobody work through their issues like we do. We swallow
abandonment and cough up independence.

You wanna scream? You see that freight train coming at you?
You havin' that lead-in-yo-legs dream again? Kick that
muthatruckin' train in its teeth and do a jig.

That's what you need. Some Mongolian Throat Singing action
and a can o' Riverdance. Unwad your drawers, Little Mama.
Let's go to the drag show.

Bust out yo corset, Sweet Ginger and show 'em all that bouillon.
We were made for the stomp. We were made out of spoon
whittlin' voodoo stew. Play those spoons, girl.

Don't let 'em take your dysfunction and turn it into a brothel.
That's YOUR dysfunction. You chop that shit up and make it
into a masterpiece. This is the year of Quit the Dumb Shit.
So, you know what that means?

Quit the dumb shit. Stop washing your pearls down
with swine. Get up off your Cadillac britches and show them motor
mouth badgers how it's done. Everything ain't gonna be alright.
Everything is going to be amazing.

GRATITUDE

To the Write Bloody Cruise Line— I am so proud to be a shipmate. So grateful for the eyes, ears and mouths of this crew. You make me want to get better at living.

The Ladies of Clementine: Hilary, Talia, Drea and Megan— Someday we will all be together again on a farm full of dusk. Thanks for teaching me turnips and letting me write about you.

Mom and Randy— I could not do this without your generous willingness to babysit and cook and lend me twenty dollars when the gas tank screams. I love you.

Kaitlin— The whole earth needs to see you. The clouds need to hold you. You are the bravest person I know. Never stop soaring over the edge.

Grom— My constant goal is to impress you. There are not enough thank you notes in the world.

JillBoom— Thank you for your massive wit and willing arms. Applesauce. Sweet Potato. Pie.

Lemon Engine— Whisky snow cones. Unbuttoned hearts. Thank you for the way you dream.

Dirt Choir: Shira, Angel, and Amy— This canoe is a spaceship. Our culture is galactic. You speak Gut fluently. I want to learn everywhere with you.

Sam Sax— Without you, this book would just be some poems. You're what the Universe was cooked in. No Homo.

Mindy Nettifee— Your name means good fairy. You are Head Cheerleader of the Good Witches. Will you drive me to all the games?

Andrea Gibson— The most comfortable nervous I have ever known. Thank you.

Rachel McKibbens— Thank you for being the mama of this community. Your leadership is changing the way we all do this. I am shaping my shoulders after you. (Also, the poem "All the Noise" is from a writing exercise on your website.)

Mahogany Browne— Thank you for believing me, for publishing my book and for being an example for single mothers everywhere. You make it all look so stunning.

Also: William Evans for sage advice, Spike for cake waffles, Melissa May for unwavering courage, Tatyana Brown for your graceful machete.

LAUREN ZUNIGA'S TOP 10 FAVORITE BOOKS

Strange Light
The *New York Times* says, "There's something that happens when you read Derrick Brown, a rekindling of faith in the weird, hilarious, shocking, beautiful power of words." This is the final collection from Derrick Brown, one of America's top-selling and touring poets. Everything hilarious and stirring is illuminated. The power of *Strange Light* is waiting.

Who Farted Wrong? Illustrated Weight Loss For the Mind
Syd Butler (of the sweet band, Les Savvy Fav) creates sketchy morsels to whet your appetite for wrong, and it will be delicious. There is no need to read between the lines of this new style of flash thinking speed illustration in this hilarious new book. Why? There are not that many lines.

New Shoes on a Dead Horse
The Romans believed that an artist's inspiration came from a spirit, called a genius, that lived in the walls of the artist's home. This character appears throughout Sierra DeMulder's book, providing charming commentary and biting insight on the young author's creative process and emotional path.

Good Grief
Elegantly-wrought misadventures as a freshly-graduated Michigan transplant, Stevie Edwards stumbles over foal legs through Chicago and kneels down to confront the wreckage of her skinned knees.

After the Witch Hunt
Megan Falley showcases her fresh, lucid poetry with a refreshing lack of jaded undertones. Armed with both humor and a brazen darkness, each poem in this book is another swing of the pick axe in this young woman's tunnel, insistent upon light.

I Love Science!
Humorous and thought provoking, Shanney Jean Maney's book effortlessly combines subjects that have previously been thought too diverse to have anything in common. Science, poetry and Jeff Goldblum form covalent bonds that put the poetic fire underneath our bunsen burners. A Lab Tech of words, Maney turns language into curious, knowledge-hungry poetry. Foreword by Lynda Barry.

Time Bomb Snooze Alarm
Bucky Sinister, a veteran poet of the working class, layers his gritty truths with street punk humor. A menagerie of strange people and stranger moments that linger in the dark hallway of Sinister's life. Foreword by Randy Blythe of "Lamb of God".

News Clips and Ego Trips
A collection of helpful articles from *Next...* magazine, which gave birth to the Southern California and national poetry scene in the mid-'90s. It covers the growth of spoken word, page poetry and slam, with interviews and profiles of many poets and literary giants like Patricia Smith, Henry Rollins and Miranda July. Edited by G. Murray Thomas.

Slow Dance With Sasquatch
Jeremy Radin invites you into his private ballroom for a waltz through the forest at the center of life, where loneliness and longing seamlessly shift into imagination and humor.

The Smell of Good Mud
Queer parenting in conservative Oklahoma, Lauren Zuniga finds humor and beauty in this collection of new poems. This explores the grit and splendor of collective living, and other radical choices. It is a field guide to blisters and curtsies.

NEW WRITE BLOODY BOOKS FOR 2012

Strange Light
The *New York Times* says, "There's something that happens when you read Derrick Brown, a rekindling of faith in the weird, hilarious, shocking, beautiful power of words." This is the final collection from Derrick Brown, one of America's top-selling and touring poets. Everything hilarious and stirring is illuminated. The power of *Strange Light* is waiting.

Who Farted Wrong? Illustrated Weight Loss For the Mind
Syd Butler (of the sweet band, Les Savvy Fav) creates sketchy morsels to whet your appetite for wrong, and it will be delicious. There is no need to read between the lines of this new style of flash thinking speed illustration in this hilarious new book. Why? There are not that many lines.

New Shoes on a Dead Horse
The Romans believed that an artist's inspiration came from a spirit, called a genius, that lived in the walls of the artist's home. This character appears throughout Sierra DeMulder's book, providing charming commentary and biting insight on the young author's creative process and emotional path.

Good Grief
Elegantly-wrought misadventures as a freshly-graduated Michigan transplant, Stevie Edwards stumbles over foal legs through Chicago and kneels down to confront the wreckage of her skinned knees.

After the Witch Hunt
Megan Falley showcases her fresh, lucid poetry with a refreshing lack of jaded undertones. Armed with both humor and a brazen darkness, each poem in this book is another swing of the pick axe in this young woman's tunnel, insistent upon light.

I Love Science!
Humorous and thought provoking, Shanney Jean Maney's book effortlessly combines subjects that have previously been thought too diverse to have anything in common. Science, poetry and Jeff Goldblum form covalent bonds that put the poetic fire underneath our bunsen burners. A Lab Tech of words, Maney turns language into curious, knowledge-hungry poetry. Foreword by Lynda Barry.

Time Bomb Snooze Alarm
Bucky Sinister, a veteran poet of the working class, layers his gritty truths with street punk humor. A menagerie of strange people and stranger moments that linger in the dark hallway of Sinister's life. Foreword by Randy Blythe of "Lamb of God".

News Clips and Ego Trips
A collection of helpful articles from *Next...* magazine, which gave birth to the Southern California and national poetry scene in the mid-'90s. It covers the growth of spoken word, page poetry and slam, with interviews and profiles of many poets and literary giants like Patricia Smith, Henry Rollins and Miranda July. Edited by G. Murray Thomas.

Slow Dance With Sasquatch
Jeremy Radin invites you into his private ballroom for a waltz through the forest at the center of life, where loneliness and longing seamlessly shift into imagination and humor.

The Smell of Good Mud
Queer parenting in conservative Oklahoma, Lauren Zuniga finds humor and beauty in this collection of new poems. This explores the grit and splendor of collective living, and other radical choices. It is a field guide to blisters and curtsies.

CPSIA information can be obtained at www.ICGtesting.com
Printed in the USA
LVOW10s0751240813

349401LV00002B/6/P